CRUEL

DIOR J. STEPHENS

CRUEL
CRUEL

DIOR J. STEPHENS

NIGHTBOAT BOOKS
NEW YORK

ISBN: 978-1-64362-158-6

Cover design by
Somnath Bhatt and Rissa Hochberger
Design and typesetting by
Rissa Hochberger and Claire Zhang
Typeset in GT Sectra

Cataloging-in-publication data is available
from the Library of Congress

Nightboat Books
New York
www.nightboat.org

TABLE OF CONTENTS

I.

ONCE AGAIN

once again,
reminded i
am not e-
nough, rough
snout stuffed
full of
pretty wisdoms,
no   outside
luster be.
/ /
once again
reminded how a
smooth seven
ain't never gon'
be no
tantalizing ten.

once again inferior to
greek statue-
esque bodies
captured in
grams un-
tethered,
sickle cell-
ular devices.
/ /
once again
flying over
occupied lands
on a
white man's
snowy dime.

once again
flashes of
tens of
putty bodies.
/ /

once again
self/ destruct,
self/ sabotage,
self/ low
deeper than
rivers of
flyover envy.

once again reminded
i nothing reminded i
ching
reminded i
worth the
worth of
half a feeble
man or, a
quarter of
one sparkling
black boy.
/ /

once again, i
expose
you, exposed,
we, all exposed,
*just below the
border line.*

once   again,
shit   goes
left, left
left, *PLIGHT,*
left, left.

/ /

once again,
feminine nails
masculine chinstrap
feminine digits
masculine i's feminine
eyes masculine
maudlin feminine
chainsaw masculine
born again, feminine.

once   again,
holding breath
like   it
owes   me
something,

                        / /

                                    once   again,
                                    wings   flap
                                    restless   dust
                                    up   in   our
                                    house   of
                                    smoke,   and
                                    ain't   shit
                                    on   fire
                                    (*escape!*).

once again,
anticipating chem
trails of yester-
year to sprinkle
over me, warm
like i've
forgotten.
/ /

once again
momma, once
again unnamed,
or, i
refuse to give
you name, feign
alzheimer's early
onset;

i know the mary ain't helping—

you hush now.

ooooooh once again
clutching diamond
ancestry. yes,
i speak
of ancestry lined
with diamonds in
ivory blood—
leone, you captive
captive—
if i
go home
when i go
home
will i
go home
do you
have a
home
for
my baggage?
/ /
once again
blink fast; big
girls don't
cry,
big boys pay
bills, fuck
bitches, get
money.

once again mind
endless, once
again scroll
infinities
            laced in
front lines; good
times, mostly
            lapsed.

                              / /
once again,
sign here,

    kiss me,

        sign here,

    kiss me,

        initial there,

rapture thee.

once again, a
language given
unto, reworked
new or, perhaps,
refurbished
direct.
/ /
once again,
*just
sayin'
some shit.*

once   again,
passing   my
red rocks.
/ /

once again, simplicity
reigns.

once again,

      once   again,

once —   again.

/ /

once   once

since   dunce

truce   flux,

carry   home.

once wailed
truest symphonies
in lowest
hell bottoms
and yet, that
nigga still ain't call me
(*flat*) back.

/ /

do you see
me *bare*,
now?

//

once again,
reminded i
am not (*more*
than
i am).

/ / / / / / / /
/ / / / / / / /
/   /   o   n   c   e
again / / / / /
/ / / / / / / /
/ / / / once / / / / again / / / /
(o n) c (e) again / / / / /
/   /   /
once / / / / /
/ again / / again / / / / /
/again / / / /
once / / / / /

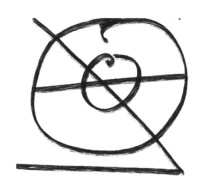

II.

CRUEL/CRUEL

04/02/2020
miscone west----

        how long does it take
           water to burn

    how   long   does it take
    water to   burn

how   long   does   it
    take   water   to   burn

how   long

        does   it
                take;
                      rioting metropoli,

           looting soot   &&
              survival sandy's,
 bleach
 mac'n'
    tires
      and   the
   FEMA   of   KATRINA—

           THIS
           ISWARTH
           ISIS-EMIC
            THISIS,

04/03/2020
H.E.S.------

two
      black
           ravens,
one
      dog,
           one
      man,
           resting
amongst
           topaz
      weeps
for
      companionship.

                  i am not
               who i am
             who was i
             who i was
          when i was;

i am the dolphin in a mask in a mask
                in plain view.

interlude
α

light-reflecting
by the
orange moon
of my
last-heart;

tell me how
the wind   chimes from
six   miles
down the   past;

feeling the
same song
sung overtime
six years
running
          running

                running—
                apollo

                      landing
          in this saturn   return,

                            a sweet picking of
                            scabs, a bright towel
                                brushed over
                                    nine-inch knife
                                            wounds,

                                            reflecting
                            strands of
                            feminine joy passed
                                    down the
                                        three-line;

tell me how
nectarfull   the forward
                   sixes
                   march,,

tell me
the prize   has upped
its elemental,,,

'til the marble tumbles and the moon sinks 'til the past passes 'til then 'til god 'til willie 'til murray 'til all the cups have been spilled—

04/08/2020
together/struction------

------------// *peach fuzz*
bugs under
gravity skin,

promise   free
clemency
on a
torrid
back
porch,

tornados
whacking touchdowns,
deranged cinderellas,
night-time manifestos
chanting

————————hope————————expired.

04/09/2020
juniper hellicopter———

sweat & musings,
tastes & slights sent
up into stratosphere
eyelashes;

        plums   like
        cherries   &
        cherries   like
        tomahawks;

                saints clad in jocks
                traps   &
                innumerable
                cloudy days;

                        liquids & oozings
                        & mucus & droplets
                        & contact & pitfalls
                        & masks & daggers;

                                hedonism   &   silent
                                charges,   fumbled
                                promises & squeaks that
                                light homes on fire.

//a silence of the hum
//a humming in the silence
//a silence in the
        humming

04/10/2020

the only thing that changes   is the floor and the weightpressed down;---

ain't sign up
for these sins,
these
l'inconnue
eyes,

prayed to the
same altars as
the masses   for

                    —teen
                    —teen

years   and   all   i   got was   a

          lifesong   that   scratches   on   repeat.

04/11/2020
howmanylicksdoesittaketilyouget------

TO
LIGHT
THE
LETHAL
TOUCH;

SILK LIKE MAGDALENE
NECTAR LIKE LEWINSKY,

TO
CRAVE
WEAPONS
OF
MASS
INSEMINATION;

FOLK LIKE BERRY
SIZZLE LIKE LONG.

interlude
β

i spill my body
languages, outwillingly,
onto your concrete
walls:

an eight count of rapture,
a falsetto for ninety
           degree   bends   and
tongues   spoken   into
themselves,

here in the
palace
of ancestral
irony,
we knock borders
until the courtyard
slips on her
nightdress,

you close the
shutters 'cause
this ain't a ritual for listening,
    it's   a   lambasting   of
every smashed piano that made
you a man, and
don't i croon for you,
              like so?
like   a   caretaker
of a   half-widened well?

trusting rim spokes cause the
syncope ain't synced in since the
sunday of half memory, lookie
here at the pot calling the kettle a
salt fiend, when you move don't
forget to leave trinkets of your
treasures with those who trifled it;

graywash mornings planning
permanent residency, residing
on lines anxious to be redrawn,
cackling fire pit forests anticipate
another hothothot! summer, the
streets cuttin' up and the lines
getting long again, frail fraughts
brought back to the shores they
exiled, a coconut with becoming
hairs, oasis of the kingdom—

11:15 am listening to
warm tones;

sun baby sent a
honeybee to
watch me from
the window but
i smashed it with
my
sting;

fear has become the
primary motive of
the categorically
denominated;

04/12/2020
wet spring howling sour eucalyptus------

we keep telling
ourselves:
hopefully   &
what's beyond
the ever/
gray?

excavating
capitalism out of
lungs like slices of
peach cobbler.

(&   &
(i have to
(believe
(there's
(many someones
(for
(every
(ones.

saw the end
of the
arroyo
& metastasized hydrangea
delirium.

shanking capitalism
out of spleens like baby b(l(ack radicals.

04/13/2020
walk the plank------

(believe in

      FEMBOY NAILS CLAWING
      UP RAFTERS OF
      HYPERCRITICALITY,
      THRICE-REMOVED.
      HOP IN SHOWER, GRAB RAVEBLUE
      SQUEEGEE,

(believe in me)

      TRY YOUR DAMNDEST
      TO SCRUBSCRUBSCRUB
      DIRT(?
      ANCESTRY(? (?
      OFF
      OF
      NECK,
      ARROW ARMS,
      MALEFICENT BIRD CHEST.

(believe in me)
(believe in me)
      (hear thy rumble
      spit! it will taste only
      of mountains and
      mantras

(BELIEVE IN
ME)
      bellowing
      untethered
      in this
      our unceasing)

04/14/2020
to be or not to be not; queerfag sweeter than moschino------

begin in reflection,
mirror possibilities,
        little biddies
staring brown-eyed in
reflection,

waltzing   home,   plastered
        to   the   moist plywood
        skin of   men   holding
        you   up   just to lay
        you
                                down.

reflection
corduroy,
corduroy
boots,
reflection of
corduroy
immaculate

slappingyou
harderthan
any
flyball.

there's still-sting
in our
gums if you glide
across them,
ever so,

reflection
         unruly,
                  tepid   &
masochistic,

         reflection   so
                  farcical
         your
         peanut
         gallery
         breaks
         oshun in
         the
         stands,

                  reflection are reflection be reflection
                              so,   so,   so,

t w o m o n t h s
     r e f l e c t i o n
        t h a t   y o u ' l l
     n e v e r
   l o o k
i n t o
   w i t h o u t
      c u e r v o
         b r a v a d o ,

deciding to think post-fissure now;

reflection in wisco-hayward
mist,

         found flowers
          wrapped
           up
           in
         jasper cases,

         reflection so
          high i
       praised mother gaia,

reflection's last
pages tumbling blindly
into an aftermath of

reflection
crisp   sierra,
            lighting
nostrils
            on
mint,

ever
green, ever
violet, ever
            rage.

reflection
            anchor into
            skin,
                    skin *crave*!
            skin   fold,
                    skin
            graph,
                    skin
            pattycake,

reflection
under
salted
shroom submarines,

raking
big   *cash*
into
brittle   bones,

trust me,
      trust baby
            reflection,

sink skin into
      reflection,

stay in church
      at least four
            hours too
                  long reflection,

hide 'n'
go get
me a
lobotomy
      reflection.

O,

sadoreflection
piratereflection
mykonosreflection
babyreflection
babyreflection—

unwrapped
        decencies

coiled
        round

your   protuberances   reflection,

            in   the name
                of the
                water
                and   the   salt
                  and the

            fever

                      reflection.

04/15/2020
untitled------

directive:

    stare into
screen
        long
enough
        for
frost
        to
mold.

    wait
        for
truth
        to
bubble
        at
your
        mouth,

firm
        &
        taciturn.

04/16/2020
strawberr------

how long you
 been standing
     there?

watching
     peep-eyed underneath
     blossom falls,
taping
     majesties to your breastplate,
     bringing   you   a lion
                         fortitude.

     will you
                light
     the
                lethal
     touch?

04/19/2020
bloodlands-----

emptying my belly
of
sin
sunshine;

tryna be
scrubbed clean.

04/26/2020
ten days-------

lately i've been
cracking memory
from bones.

interlude
γ

it's three thirty
five p-
m it's three
forty   five   pm,

and if i drop the
craft-cicle i
might just
admit this
lock and key,

obtusify the
eye until seeds
open
their
diaphragms—

time is no longer
of the essence;

a sweetness
lost at midday sun;

a knot of affections;

three whispers and a
bell in the background;

always something there;
always something peaking above the bridge;

04/27/2020

we cried together-------

                    HOLDING
             MELTED
      NIGHTS;

                             LABORING,

                             LABORING, &

                             LOOKING OUT OF THE

                             SAME GODDAMN WINDOWS!

04/29/2020
savage pink lemonade‑‑‑‑‑‑‑

SLURPEE STRAWS TYPING OUT HALF-ASSED STORIES OF WATERED-DOWN TOMORROW, SMELLING PORK RINDS, SMELLING SALT, CRYSTALS IN HOLES UNIDENTIFIED, FLOATING, SPEAKING OF BLACK SILK EBULLIENCE.

FRAMING FANS AND BLOWING CHARCOAL, CRUSTING OVER THE EYES OF NORMALCY — I SEE THE QUALMS OF THUNDER IN THE STREETS! LICK MY CHARGED SANDSTORM & PRONOUNCE STILLNESS AS MY MOTHER.

DREAMING OF RED WINE VALLEYS, A WORLD WITHOUT DISEASE, POISONS OF THE SOIL. CROCHETING TUMBLEWEEDS INTO CLAY POTS & SINKING TEETH INTO CHLOROFORM.

FEELING MYSELF SOFT,
    GREEN WAVE, FEELING MYSELF
            GOD'S GREEN LIGHT.

interlude
δ

——all that
just to
start a poem
for the new
moon of my
orange moon;

i offer a
puzzle
that will
madden you,
but your ego
feeds
differently;

repulsive namesake for a
bloodlust lovelust; the ratcheting
of the innards; the deathhorn
blows again; swerving in/out
of intersectionality; giddy as a
glumful of glee feasting on
dropdown rainbows;

a poet is a poem is a keeper

thinking fawkes
had the
right idea;

thinking fawkes
as north
star
cause
liberation
never came
before
a
few

never came before a few fireworks
but i've sicked dogs on men in
white / / a wave swirling mind
membranes just to turn my head
toward the flame for a bell longer;

———

(just to) *turn* *my* *flame* *for* *a* *bell* *longer,* **like** revolution's last chance;

III.

UNTITLED
YELLOW
PAGES
1-12

UYP 1

style quick checks over
clip-staple coal over
chopper/less blue
skies over
      a summer of endless inferno,
          rockets, and artillery.

aghast with
sycophantic notions,
black iliad's
pour from   activized,
catalized
        sensation—

   & the ghost rivers of harlem

   play light patches

   in your good ear.

              sitting
              sideways
              in gold rush,
              downloading
      mental schematics for
      what once   was
      natural——————————didn't get to see blue
                              jezebel as she flew by, again.

raven,
     call him   SUNSET   ca-caws   five   times   in
solidarity   for the homies—
       call   it   ECONEGRO,

          still,   no blacks in the
    YUBA,
   only nude
   lily-whites
       and eight-ball
      peacocks———————   STILL,
                       there's a hope in
               the wind that slants
                   pessimism.

UYP 2

                    a
candle holding
revolutionary
hands;
        six   clown   cars
        with   hornet's
        nests
                up top.

                    beating
            kkwaenggwari,
                janggu;

        the might of two
                        swells
                    smashing chalk
                            on $82k/year.

open your windows,   *loren.*

why
aren't
you
                    home,
loren?

what
hillside view blasts
decency out of frame,,

dreaming of
being heard,

dreaming of being
bit down on by
loose ties,—

**WE NEVER
DREAMT THIS
SUMMER,**

and yet,

lady
june blows
prideful as
the people
beat the
street,

    horns honk
    from dusk
    til dawn,

    firecracker encores
    every
        night,

           a summer of
                old
                  jack
                   and jasmine
                  in   the
                    backyard,

    undreamt,,

                          unheard (of),

asking all masks of capital and colonial be removed
before we come to the lord my lord our lord none of it
matters *inshallah* say 52 hail mary's for your ancestors lost
in uncharted, unfriendly waters, throw your back out in prayer
for they see you as your blood *inshallah* sing hymnals at the feet of
mules, tell them change is the latest alternative milk trend — s o a k
t h a t   s h i t   r i g h t   u p   *inshallah* praise be & benedict your altered
gaze, reconstructed eyes & fickle tongue *inshallah* honor your
blessings for a fortnight & wash your hair in red clay *inshallah* try to
wash all the masks off of you now *inshallah* still your whitest parts
into a bowl — fingernails, teeth, eye-whites; combine with chicken
wishbone, broken, a hefty serving of onyx fragments & one marvin
gaye record, also broken *inshallah* ask that whiteness to reevaluate
& see thy onyx, thou heartiest & solemnest of stones *inshallah* ask,
why be anything less? sing to mama lucy unearthed — say *inshallah*
grandmother; i long for your essence of black purity in all that i am,,,

outside of
art i see
thyself
        unearthed,   humming
holies into the wind,
spieling rhythms
of hot-cross-
tongues,

        rake your ashes into the streets &
        make a white man cry at
        the
        waterfall of
        their
        exception.

coughing up
grime-
disturbia,
        sun-spotting
black hoodies as
angels of resurrection;
        cross out every year of
                expected death— plant
        plum trees in your
                white neighbor's backyard & say:

                all that
                hangs
                here is
                more
                than
                        gold.

feather michael sat down on my
shoulder as 826 fireworks
popped for floyd five weeks in a
row — michael sat on shoulder
as trumpets trumpeted up the
sonic river — crying & bellowing
— *i who am nothing — nothing,*
who am i — show me the way to
the proper p's — *prosperity —*
peace — plenty — michael floats
round cranium in — blue blue
light — says — i must learn to
follow before i can lead — &
there in the 5252 cerulean — i
flew to the mountain of apex
consciousness — uncertain in my
feathers — wings clipped long
ago — still slaying one then two
— floating upstream in western
paradise.

i.

PLUM HONEY PLUM SMOOTH PLUM OVERABUNDANCE
PLUM SPIRAL PLUM MERITOCRACY PLUM HAY BEETLE
PLUM WEIGHT OF ALL PLUM OVERTURNED REINSTATED
REDEFINED PLUM SHIVER LIKE HONEYBEES PLUM SASHAY
IN THE GOLD SWAT PLUM INTERRUPTION FROM THE SUB/
DIMENSION PLUM RUTABAGA PLUM SACRIFICE ON MOLE
HILL PLUM BELIEF THAT ONE DAY THE SIGNS WILL BE
CLEAR AS FROST PLUM FIRE FISH LIKES NOTHING RAW
PLUM FOOL PLUM IRONY PLUM MEAT THAT GRINDS AND
REDEFINES PLUM SUFFRAGE FOR AN OVERDUE SPRING
PLUM HONEYSUCKLE PLUM PLUM WHAT WASTE IS IMPLICIT
IN FRUITION PLUM MIGHT PLUM DIRECT HOLY PLUM HOLY
PLUM HOLY,,,,,,,,,,,,,,,,,,,,,,,

ii.

pretending at something,
plum split open,
purple puss—

        playing computer,
        pillowing
              dry
        palm,

praying sideways,
praying more,

           cause

possibly

pirouetting up riptides
    with a
pumpkin headed
prissy-boy
pristine in
painted neon,

pretending &
polling & proclivities &

next time won't
promise as much.

laying lines in
capitalized, demoralized
shores,
hoping hands
full of curses
softball a
hail mary
clemency my way.

towers,
hayrides   &
damnation
!
is there enough
yet?
enough delilah sunshade left to bemoan?

a whole bottle to myself as i accept pre-diagnosis;
breaking up with the bear of my heart; long licking
callouses of ten gemini seasons; stalling nightshade
roses for sleep;;;

UYP 9

flyby brandy; mixed callouses asking for a highball; just; chatting politics;
just; listening to white cries on black parades; just lifting lug-legs-dumbells-
round-my-jim-crow-ankles; just sliding; just assembling roses for the next
funeral i won't be able to attend; just;

when you feel the need for heart palpitations
just
step outside.

---

just enhancing my
melanin; just;
wondering where
god drinks; just;
having another; an;
other other; off day;
just; breathing in dragon;
steaming out snow; just
slow breaths——

/*poet of*
the current! how do you swim?

we don't.

just brothers i'll never meet;
just brothers tryna see sunrise;
just clouds; just rampage;
just; liberation looting;
just fucking turn off the tv;
just silence; *respite for us*;
just; silence;

you;
where is your;
just-voice?

told myself i'd sit
outside today as
long
as necessary but the
whole block is hot
with grieving;

shovels scooped up
full of dog shit;
peach trees pitying
their blisters;

can only depend on
the sun as much as i
depend on black
death; which is to
say;
   with utmost
certainty; just a
small chance;
small;
of absolute
obliteration;

to dream past the past of
shackle men and
liberation lost. to
dream in black neon.
looking back long ago,
wearing visors for vision
scars; seeing the unseen
and undocumented.

loosening lassos on
ancestry like unraveled
fruit-by-the-foot. veins
protruding up 'n' out of
aberdeen skin, glistening
ivory coast spirit. to think
not of shackles broken, but
of a time before. rewriting
history to see theirself in it.
a land before time or a time
before land or property or gazes.

flowing into futures of black uprising
and bloodbath cherry streets. to
see a future with violence; restorative.
feigning no outline of peace — sangin'
we shall overcome with automatics tucked in
arm; black fists raised. to not see
any more fourths, nan more -olumbuses'. just
me and huey and ms. davis shooting the
shit after shooting some —————————

seeing a new type of first contact.
one devoid of erasure,
one rife with life spittle. genuflect
& reconnected to a vision, most high
(*inshallah*). laying purple reefs royal,
cross unshackled, exalted ankles;

still hullabaloos swaying up like lost
ballots. to sow the reaping and taste
moss on your fingertips. sprinkling
uncertainty with generosity & pinging
onyx over alabaster. take three steps to
your left and grab everyone into the fold.
stolen truths cost a smooth tree ninety-nine
when your time is up.

sitting honest with self, slowly, my roux ever-burning.
tell me sweetness on the solstice.
summer begat spring begat winter begat ——

i know of no new beginnings,
rudimentary in hope,
palm leaves cover my eyes
from centuries of dismay.

      is this harkening in my soul the call that i've been waiting
      for? one more chance for sanctity? awash in bacon grease
      and crystallized syrups of dangerous beauty.
      unleashed into high-line sierras, whisked flat with
          bounteous mercy.

not talking much today
simply painting with my
breathstrokes, summer
lounging with creatures
with english names. tumble
butterfly, zipline ladybug;
are we one and the same?
branded with names from
languages we did not speak
by tyrants who looked
nothing like
us.

not talking much today,
simply watching [   ]
play with proximity to the
unknown. thinking about
rainbow road years lost under
men who looked nothing like
us.

not talking much today, simply
calling my own bluff,
not running starry-jeweled-teary-
eyed to the corner store, not
giving nobody who does not look
like us any coin for my poison.

not talking much today,
          just asking the sun to still.

UYP 12

wanna write in this gold while it lasts,
see: where i live,
my very breath
is my damnation.

wanna sit in this gold and talk a while,
to the She we all believe
should be.

wanna ignore your texts and
snag-bite double-time on raw lip.

wanna wear scandalous skivvies
for an audience of one.

wanna see Floyd
breathing and
don't wanna talk about it.

wanna stop feeling;

white gaze white gaze.

wanna be religion-
less, since
     no god we know of
makes
     sense of this.

wanna slide locks open
with my pinky nail,
surprise bamboo men
     with my ladylike
          shrine of
          pulled split ends
          &
          still
          don't wanna
               talk about it.

wanna give
every black body
a medal—
             &
      a collection of
        plastic bags
        from under
          the sink
          (*you'll need*
           them)

wanna give respite, yet,
  instead, biting raw lips to
   mimic violence.

   stomping on revenge's pudgy toes is the only

   cleansing I know—

wanna see
smooth
skies
lined,

wanna see
twist be-
come *shout*.

Acknowledgements

A huge thanks to the following publications who have given some of these poems a home. Thank you to Untitled Writing, where "Juniper Hellicopter" first appeared. Thank you to Peach Mag for first publishing "UYP 3" and "UYP 4." Thank you to Marías at Sampaguitas for first publishing "4/29/20 savage pink lemonade".

Mom, thank you for always lifting me up. For believing in the artist in me before anyone else. For your unyielding love. Thank you to my Ronnie, my Eric D., my Ma—my main team for life, my biggest cheerleaders.

Ronnie, Eric, thank you for reading and encouraging my work from the beginning until now—y'all are my best friends (but you can delete those early, early writings now, *please*).

A never-ending thank you to the village of Black women that it took to raise this once-upon-a-child. To Lorraine, to Beulah, to Ms. Murray, and countless more. I owe everything to y'all.

A supreme amount of gratitude to the friends who keep my spirit alight: Briana Phillips, Emma Ladji, Taylor Byas, Eva Hoffman, Brandon Logans, and many others whose love keeps this fish alive and swimming.

A huge thank you to Tonya M. Foster for being a mentor, a confidant, and a dear, dear beloved.

To Trisha Low, your belief in this work has meant the world to me. I will forever be thankful to have had you as the editor of this project.

To Rita Bullwinkel, your eyes on the early drafts gave me so much hope and confidence. Thank you for your enthusiastic yeses to all of my wildest ideas.

To Gia, Lindsey, Stephen, and the Nightboat team, I couldn't have ever imagined a more fitting press for this book. From the bottom of my dolphin heart, thank you all so very much, for everything.

To Uncle Willie, I love you forever.

To little Dior writing poems in his room who would've never imagined a moment like this. To the Dior that didn't see past twenty-seven. To the Dior past, present, and future who ever doubts himself: never forget the love that made and keeps you.

To the Black, queer writers who've blazed the hell out of the trail before me: I honor you. I thank you. Thank you for constantly reminding me that we are not as alone as the world wants us to think. This one's for y'all, forever.

DIOR J. STEPHENS is a proud Midwestern Pisces poet. He is the author of *SCREAMS & lavender, 001*, and *CANNON!*. Dior holds an MFA in Creative Writing from California College of the Arts and is currently a doctoral candidate in the Philosophy program at the University of Cincinnati. Dior hopes to be a dolphin in his next life. Dior's preferred pronouns are he/they. They tweet at @dolphinneptune and Instagram at @dolphinphotos

NIGHTBOAT BOOKS

Nightboat Books, a nonprofit organization, seeks to develop audiences for writers whose work resists convention and transcends boundaries. We publish books rich with poignancy, intelligence, and risk. Please visit nightboat.org to learn about our titles and how you can support our future publications.

The following individuals have supported the publication of this book. We thank them for their generosity and commitment to the mission of Nightboat Books:

Kazim Ali
Anonymous (4)
Abraham Avnisan
Jean C. Ballantyne
The Robert C. Brooks Revocable Trust
Amanda Greenberger
Rachel Lithgow
Anne Marie Macari
Elizabeth Madans
Elizabeth Motika
Thomas Shardlow
Benjamin Taylor
Jerrie Whitfield & Richard Motika

This book is made possible, in part, by grants from the New York City Department of Cultural Affairs in partnership with the City Council and the New York State Council on the Arts Literature Program.